ICONS OF THE PASSIO

ICONS
OF THE PASSION

A Way of the Cross

W. H. VANSTONE

Illustrations by SHEILA WRIGLEY

DARTON·LONGMAN+TODD

First published in Great Britain in 1985 by
Mayhew McCrimmon Ltd
This edition published in 2000 by

Darton, Longman and Todd Ltd
1 Spencer Court
140–142 Wandsworth High Street
London SW18 4JJ

ISBN 0–232–52357–6

A catalogue record for this book is available from the British Library.

Designed by Sandie Boccacci
Phototypeset in 11½/15pt Goudy by
Intype London Ltd
Printed and bound in Great Britain by
Halstan & Co Ltd, Amersham, Bucks

FOREWORD

Canon Vanstone was one of the most thoughtful and original of modern British theologians. He published little but his remarkable parish sermons, cathedral addresses, and retreat meditations for clergy and religious orders gathered many devoted followers from every walk of life. These meditations are a precious illustration of his style.

To understand the Christian faith, he insists, we need to attend and wait, ready to receive whatever the Christian story has to disclose to us. This is not mindless. There are questions to be asked, ambiguities to be sorted out; but there is no artificial division between devotional and theological understanding. To receive a religious meaning one must hear the story, read the poem, listen to the music, or attend to the work of the artist. These powerful icons and the thoughts that accompany them do not allow us the easy assertion that suffering, though unacceptable to us, is willed by God and therefore for the best. They speak to us of a God who, while author of the world's being, yet shares in all our agonies. Bonhoeffer said, 'Only a suffering God can help.' That is the mystery to which we are invited to attend and to receive.

ROBERT RUNCIE

INTRODUCTION

Around the walls of the chapel of the Community of St Peter at Horbury hang the Icons of the Passion, carved by Sister Sheila during 1980 and 1981.* These icons at first move the observer to think rather than to feel. Feeling will follow thought; but their first challenge is that we should think, reflect and connect.

I have no right to an opinion on Sister Sheila's skill or technique as a woodcarver; but I discern an interpretation of Jesus' Passion to which I cannot but assent. So I count it a privilege to be allowed to set beside each icon my own meditation. The meditation is in no way a summary or precis in words of what the artist is saying in the tougher medium of wood: her meaning is to be received only by looking attentively at the icon itself. The meditation is offered in each case only as a hint of, or pointer to, what the icon and, through it the artist herself, may be saying.

W. H. VANSTONE

* The icons now hang in the Church of St Thomas, Kirkholt, Lancashire.

ONE

All lovers come at last to Gethsemane, and wait there for the outcome of their loving. Loving itself is a beginning, an invitation, an offering: for the receiving which it invites but does not compel love can only wait, and to wait no longer is to cease to love.

For the receiving or the rejection, the understanding or the misunderstanding, the loving or the grudging response, love must wait: and the intensity of the waiting is the measure of the loving. As He waits who is the all-loving, the sweat falls like drops of blood; and His hands tremble as they reach up to take and receive the cup of the world's response.

What is in the cup cannot be seen. But because He does not cease to love, He will wait for whatever comes. His hands will always be upraised to receive and take to Himself whatever is mixed in the cup which contains the world's response.

TWO

There is no going back now. The world has taken over, and hurries Him about from place to place according to its own programme.

Is this really His scene? Was it for this that He came into the world – to be pushed and pulled around in this ridiculous way, as custom required or politicians decided?

Was it for this that *I* gave my loyalty to Him – to get trapped in these trivial things that are now expected and required of me? 'Meetings and money, keeping the rules, running the playgroup, bearing with fools. . .' Surely the role of a Christian in the world should be more distinct and elevated than this?

But notice that, as well as the constraining rope which pulls Him here and there, there is a goad or spear which drives Him forward. Perhaps its shaft, which we do not see, is the shaft of His own love. It is that which makes Him 'leadable'. It is His love which drives Him into and through a scene which is not His own. He could withdraw from that inappropriate scene only by ceasing to love.

THREE

His back is offered to the smiters, His long-suffering to gratuitous abuse.

The thongs of the lash are curiously suggestive of tubes draining the strong body or the roots of an alien growth feeding upon its strength. The gratuitous cruelty of the scourging hints at evil as a parasite, fastening itself on His exposure, nourishing itself by His patience.

There is something in us, in our sin, which, because He does not strike back, will strike yet more savagely, lash yet more bitterly: there is an anger which feeds and swells upon non-resistance.

But there is a limit to anger, a point at which its sated and swollen bulk is vented and collapses into shame. But there is no limit to His long-suffering. When anger, bitterness and resentment have collapsed, He will still be there.

FOUR

The robe of royal purple in which He is dressed by the soldiers does not fit: it is too large: it is not His own. But it is not the mocking soldiery alone who dress Him in ill-fitting robes of earthly power: so also, in art and imagination, do some of those who believe in Him. Because they believe also in the primacy of power, they attribute to Him the trappings of power and adorn Him with its symbols: then, while showing respect to Him, they can continue to worship power and take pride and satisfaction in their own power.

But the robe which belongs to Him, His own robe, is that 'dying crimson' which 'like a robe spreads o'er His body on the Tree': it is the robe of life poured out, of power expended, of self given in love. It is the wearer of *this* robe that we must learn to worship.

A saint in his cell was visited by a radiant figure in a gorgeous robe who announced himself as Christ returned to earth and called for the saint's worship. But the saint said: 'I will not believe that He has returned to earth until I see Him in the form and robe wherein He suffered.' Thereupon the figure faded, and the saint recognised its appearing as his last and most subtle temptation.

FIVE

It is a strong figure who bears the Cross: but its weight is commensurate with His strength. It is the weight of the world. Because He loves the world, the world is a great matter to Him: it weighs upon Him, bears upon Him, as the object of love always bears upon the lover. In His bearing of the heavy Cross we discern with what weight His beloved world bears upon Him.

He does not hold the world in His hands like a toy or dangle it from His fingers. He is not the puppet-master but Atlas. The powerful shoulders are bowed, the body strained to retain the balance.

'Underneath are the everlasting arms' . . . but such is the weight of His beloved world that those arms are tensed and exerted to the limit of their strength . . . 'Here is God, whose arms of love aching, spent, the world sustain.'

SIX

Tradition has it that He fell under the weight of the Cross: but the icon suggests rather rest, recuperation, the re-gathering of His strength. If He fell, it was to rise again and continue on His way.

He will not fail. His strength, His resourcefulness, will suffice to bear and sustain whatever is laid upon Him – whatever, through loving the world, He lays upon Himself. His strength is sufficient for Him, and therefore for us.

But we are not to think that a measure of His strength is always held in reserve, held back from the world and its needs, kept to Himself as His own security. Rather we are to think that at every moment all that He has is expended for the world's needs . . . yet, whenever the world needs more, He will gather more to give.

SEVEN

Close to the earth, close to His beloved world, He gathers strength to continue on His way. The figure who stands beside Him is simply *there*: she does nothing but is deliberately there. She assists, but only in the exact (etymological) sense of 'standing near'. She cannot alleviate the weight of the world – for she is part of the world. She cannot augment His strength – for all her strength is derived from His. Yet it is very important that she should be there, offering her presence: to Him who gives Himself for her no offering is more appropriate than that she should be with Him, standing beside Him.

Who is this figure standing beside Him? Is she Mary? Or Veronica? Is she the Church? Or the world at prayer? Is she perhaps whoever looks at the icon with respect and gratitude and love?

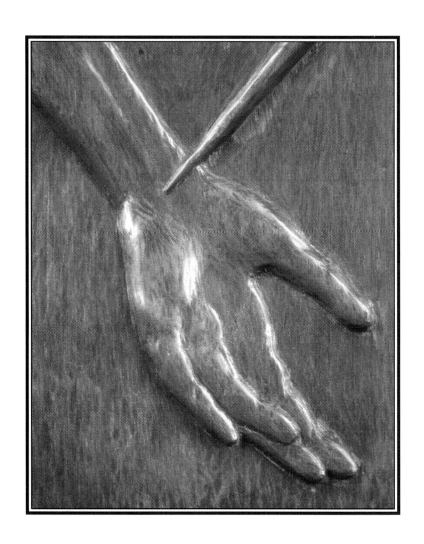

EIGHT

The nail entering the wrist is as sharp and fine as a needle: it pins Him as a butterfly is pinned. It enters Him not with brute force but with subtle precision: it is a refined outrage, the infliction and wound of a sophisticated world.

In the days of His flesh He flinched less from the vulgar sins of harlots and extortioners than from the suave offences of the enlightened: less, one might say, from violence in the streets than from vindictiveness in the cloister or the common room. The finely polished needle, designed to repair what is torn and relieve what is pained, may become the instrument of the most cruel outrage.

NINE

Again He is not alone: but now we are certain who, in a historical sense, the figures are – Mary and John.

They are at the level of His feet: standing under Him: in a literal sense understanding Him. They wait, attentive to receive whatever He may say or express or disclose. They offer not only their physical presence but also their receptivity, their openness, their attention.

They do not ask questions, or offer advice or comfortable words: they simply wait upon His words, and, whatever His words are, they will receive them. This is the role and service of an understanding person – to receive, take in, absorb whatever it is that another wishes or needs to disclose.

It is not easy to understand. Certainly it is not easy to understand Him – it never has been. Now, in this most difficult time, Mary and John need each other's support as they watch and wait for whatever He may disclose.

TEN

The artist does not show the face of the Crucified: nor do the writers of the Gospels. In the earlier part of their story they have told us much about the thoughts and feelings, the love and grief and indignation, that could be read in His face: but now they are silent about these matters. The artist also is silent: she shows us only the slumped head crowned with thorns.

In the face there would be unspeakable pain: pain beyond expression in words or paint or carved wood. Perhaps it is for this reason that the face is concealed. Or perhaps it is concealed so that our feelings may be spared. But perhaps it is for a deeper reason that our eye is drawn not to the pained face but to the slumped head and the spent and drained body. For it is not through the pain that was inflicted on Him that He is our Saviour, but through the totality of His self-expenditure, of His self-giving. He gives Himself for the world 'unto death': until He is drained: until there is no more to give. He loves us and all the world not with measured and limited benevolence but 'unto death'. Therein lies our hope and the world's salvation.

ELEVEN

The day's work is done. The nails have done their cruel work and are laid aside. The sponge and the ladder have done their gracious work and are laid aside. All has been done to His body that the world willed to do, and it is laid to rest.

The cup which He took into His hands in Gethsemane is empty now. It has been drained. He has received, taken into Himself, all that was contained in the cup of the world's response to His love. He took it into His hands in Gethsemane not knowing what it might contain: now He has drained it to the dregs and knows its bitter taste. The cup is empty now and falls to the ground.

So it seems at first. But the strong lines of the ladder, the reed and the two parallel nails persuade the eye that, as the cup falls, it is moving away from the Cross and towards the sealed opening of the sepulchre. There at the opening it will be when the Sabbath is over and the seal is broken and the Crucified comes forth: and He will again take it into His hands and receive whatever is mixed in it. For it is the cup of the world's response: and, until that day when He ceases to love the world, He who ever lives will receive endlessly, the cup of rejection or of answering love which the world has mixed for Him.

And the day when He ceases to love the world will never come.

TWELVE

The breaking of the bread is seen as its *opening* rather than as its fragmentation. It is through being opened that the bread becomes broken: it is because He opens His heart that it becomes a broken heart.

He who is our bread, the bread of life, is broken upon the Cross. He is broken by the sin of the world. But he can be broken only because, of His own will, He is laid open, exposed, vulnerable. Of His own will He loves the world; and therefore He gives to the world a certain power over Himself – power to bring joy or grief, weal or woe. So of His own will He opens His heart to whatever the world may do.

On Maundy Thursday He discloses the meaning of what will happen on Good Friday. He opens the bread, and says: 'This is my Body' and places it in men's hands; and men are free to treat it with grateful reverence or with indifference and contempt. He opens the bread: and thereby He discloses that it is of His own will and because of His own love that He will be exposed and vulnerable on Good Friday.

In His self-opening we discern the measure of His love: it is without limit or reserve or qualifications: He loves the world 'unto death'. Therefore in His body broken on the cross we discern the world's salvation, and in the opened, broken bread we receive the bread of life.